ETERNITY
FOR A
MIST

ETERNITY
FOR A
MIST

ADVENTURES WITH GOD
THROUGH JAIL MINISTRY

JEFF TREPTOW

XULON ELITE

Xulon Press Elite
2301 Lucien Way #415
Maitland, FL 32751
407.339.4217
www.xulonpress.com

Paperback ISBN-13: 978-1-66286-887-0
Hard Cover ISBN-13: 978-1-66286-888-7
Ebook ISBN-13: 978-1-66286-889-4

Preface

I wrote this book because I couldn't contain my feelings or zealous passion for our eternal Holy God. I have to tell the world about our God and Father and His supernatural, boundless love for us. Something unexpected happened while writing this book, I became intimately close to our infinite Creator. I also realized an incredible reality that stopped me in a whirlwind of thought...we Christians are in the royal family of our infinite and loving God forever! I tried my best in this book to describe God, who simply put, is indescribable. He is a Supernatural Being that is at a level so far superior to a human being, it is impossible to describe Him within the limits of the English language and my mere mortal mind. *1 Timothy 6:16 says, "Who alone is immortal and who lives in unapproachable light, whom no one has seen or can see. To Him be honor and might forever. Amen".* It's quite remarkable that God, given the magnitude of His lofty magnificence, allows me to even attempt to write about Him. Only through help from His Holy Spirit can I hope to capture a glimmer of His graceful majesty in the pages of this book, but here it goes......

Table of Contents

Chapter 1

How I Got Off The Bench
And Into The Game

I was getting through life just fine while achieving, accomplishing, and experiencing lots of the "normal things". I had earned a college degree, I was raising young children with my wife, I had a good job and a home, I had relationships with friends and family, I was attending social events and parties, and I was attending church. I thought I was doing great, until *that* one Sunday in church. The pastor was speaking passionately that day about living our lives differently, living life for God and His glorious plan. It hit me hard that Sunday while sitting in church, that I never really did anything for God at all. Sunday church felt like sitting on the bench while the world outside of the church building felt like the big game. I believed that God existed, but nothing in my life showed any evidence of it. Something stirred inside me that day because I had this longing to do something great for God, but I always seemed way too busy, distracted or too tired to actually do something, and I also wasn't sure what to do or how to get started. But that Sunday was a major turnaround for me, and something was triggered inside of me. It was time to do something; any-thing really. I finally acted upon this desire deep within me to serve the supreme, omnipotent God. I decided to get off the bench and into the game. I started thinking of things and then started doing things to please God. I did simple things like giving out food and drinks to the hungry on the streets of Los Angeles, taking items to the homeless center, offering my garage to a homeless person to get off the streets, caring for those in need, and going on short mission trips to orphanages in Mexico. As I did more for God, I started to understand the scripture and appreciate the beauty of God's words in *Acts 20:35, "Its more blessed to give than to receive".* God intended for us, before the creation of the universe, to do good works that bring Glory to Him, not to ourselves. We are called to spread God's word, and to make disciples of men. I can't describe to you the profound feeling that giving to others has brought into my life, there is nothing like it! Even the most desperate and hopeless people on the streets were so kind and appreciative of even the smallest of items that I gave them. The love that I experienced from the little children in the orphanages in Mexico was super-natural and deeply moving to me and almost impossible to describe. I started to understand that God had blessed me with resources so that I could, in turn, give to others. How special I felt that God chose me to bring blessings to those in need. It made me feel so warm and close to God and I gained wisdom. I learned that life is not about accumulating material objects for myself. *Matthew 6:33 says, "But seek first*

His kingdom and His righteousness, and all these things will be given to you as well." God has most certainly been true to His word in my life! He has richly blessed my life to a level that I could have never imagined! He also sent His son to earth to give up His life for me. Because of this, I continue to seek God and His kingdom out of love for Him. When we do the things that we were created to do, it brings a wave of passionate contentment into our lives and more importantly, a personal connection directly to God Himself, the God that created all that exists. This contentment comes from the fact that we are living the lives that God intended for us before time began. We are doing what we were created to do. It's something that is profoundly spiritual and wonderfully warm. It makes me sad when I hear others belittle God's blessings by comparing themselves to someone that is financially better off than they are and then complain about how little they have. They don't even realize the depth of what God has done for them and they don't even seem grateful for what God has given them. They look down on others who are not super-rich and consider them as failures in life. But thankfully, God doesn't judge us by the house we live in or how much money we have in our bank account, He looks directly at our hearts. My daily life improved immensely once I understood my purpose and was living it out. God created a world full of opportunities for us to bring glory to Him. He strategically placed me close to Los Angeles, where not only is the need so great, but I am also only a few hours drive from Mexico, where the need is far greater.

All we need to do is step out of our comfortable world and step into the world that God has set before us.

One day, while at work, my friend Dennis and I were casually talking in my office. Somehow, our conversation drifted towards church and serving God. He asked me if I was interested in joining his jail ministry team. There was something about Dennis that came across very authentic and wonderfully genuine. I asked him how long he had been going into jail and serving, "about 17 years," he told me. I was blown away at his commitment! "This guy is the real deal," I thought to myself, "Seventeen years, wow!" Dennis is a true warrior for God, humbly serving in jail for all these years! I wanted to step up my game and God placed this new opportunity before me. The timing couldn't have been more perfect, God had prepared me for this moment. "Sure, I'm interested," I told him. The next day at work, Dennis handed me a simple form to fill out. A few weeks later, he excitedly told me, "You're in! You start this Sunday!" And so began my journey into the world of jail ministry.

Chapter 2

Living For A Higher Purpose, Not Ourselves

How cool it is to be living for a higher purpose, the ultimate, highest purpose a human being can attain, to be a messenger and warrior for God! Since starting jail ministry, I seem to have the deepest conversations with the inmates. Even though they often call it "church", our ministry sessions in jail are quite different because we have biblical reading along with group discussion as well as continuous question-and-answer. It feels like maybe God is using me as that "one last chance" for them. It's a little scary, that God trusts me, an untrained counselor, to fulfill such a critical role. Could I do this by myself? No, but I have found that with God, anything is possible. *Matthew 19:26 says, "Jesus looked at them and said, 'With man this is impossible, but with God all things are possible.'"* Sadly, many people today are living the distracted life that I did for so many years, with no purpose at all. Instead of doing things for our own selfish desires or fulfillment, why not do something for God and make life spectacular? Why not live to the highest level and reach for the heavens? Do not settle for mediocrity in your life, serve and strive to please our Father, and see what happens. We must ensure that love for God and for our fellow men and women are our ultimate drivers in life. I have to admit that it's been fascinating for me to experience miracles from God, behind jail walls, as I watch criminals becoming Christians. I don't know how many times the inmates have been astonished that the very topic I chose to discuss that particular Sunday was either something they had just prayed about or something that had been recently weighing heavy on their hearts. The most violent criminals wear red wristbands in jail and being locked in a small room with them, with no guard in the room, is not the most comfortable situation at times, but it exhilarates me to be intimately close to an uncontainable God! God doesn't need me to help Him run the earth or the universe, but he cares about me so deeply that he wants me to be and allows me to be in direct participation with His planned work. What a rush! This is something far greater than anything this world can ever offer. It's like being in an action-adventure movie, but it's real life. The things this world offers: houses, cars, vacations, money, drugs, alcohol, and sex, pale in comparison to the eternal life and unparalleled joy that God freely gives. *John 10:28-30 says, "I give them eternal life, and they shall never perish…. no one can snatch them out of my Father's hand."* There is much comfort in those words, , no one can snatch us from our Father's hand, but many may try. I've met some of the most interesting and authentic people that I know through the relationships I have developed through my Christian faith, particularly with those that serve God through ministry work. The people working humbly in the trenches, those that are missionaries, working in jails, helping the orphans , helping the homeless, and caring for widows, all doing the hard work for God. This is faith and action working hand-in-hand, just like it says in *James 2:14, "What good is it, my brothers, if a man claims to have faith but has no deeds?" James 2:26 "As the body without the spirit is dead, so faith without deeds is dead."* I was listening to a pastor on Christian radio one morning and he was making the point that unpaid volunteers can have a greater impact in the ministry world (more so than formal pastors or priests) because people realize that the volunteer's motivation comes from something different. The volunteer's passion, faith and love are what motivates them from their heart and this does not involve money at all. This forces people to ponder a little bit and wonder what motivates a volunteer to do what they do. Faith is not merely going to church for an hour every Sunday, but instead, it involves daily actions that demonstrate our trust and faith in God along with daily sacrifices for our Creator out of love for Him. It's the best way to live, no doubt about it. It truly is living the dream, living for the Master of the endless universe! It seems that many people spend an entire lifetime trying to figure out what this life on earth is all about, what does it all mean? Here are Jesus' last words before ascending into heaven: *Matthew 28:18-20, "Then Jesus came to them and said "All authority in heaven and on earth has been given to me. Therefore, go and make disciples of all nations, baptizing them in the name of the Father and of the Son and of the Holy Spirit, and teaching them to obey everything I have commanded you. And surely I am with you always, to the very end of the age."* This is why we're all here, to make disciples of all mankind and to teach others to obey the commands of Jesus which includes baptism. Through the power of God, we can have an impact on others that will reach far beyond this earthly life into the realms of eternity. This mission for God has brought deep and rich purpose to my life. Sharing my faith in jail, among the inmates, has allowed me to use and develop my spiritual gift of teaching. I originally went into jail ministry thinking that I would help others, but I often find that I am helping myself and that I learn from the inmates as much as they learn from me. One of the members of my jail ministry team is a licensed attorney in New York as well as Washington D.C., and he interrupted his law career and a healthy income to become a student at Master's Seminary in southern California. "What made you step away from your law practice?" I asked. "Unjust outcomes of some of the law suits I was involved with left me demoralized and disheartened," he explained. "There was one unjust lawsuit in particular that really got to me. It involved a helicopter accident in which two people were killed. I was raised in the traditional church but wasn't finding answers there. I met some Christian friends a few years after the helicopter trial ended, and they were living their lives differently than anything I had seen before. They frequently quoted the bible, which kind of annoyed me at first, but over time, I found that they were not living life the world's way and that caught my interest. They were authentic, and it reminded me that my mom had always told me that each one of us is here on earth for a specific reason. I look back now, and I feel that even back then, God was shaping me for jail ministry. Jesus words in *Matthew 6:19-21* are always on my mind *'Do not store up for yourselves treasures on earth, where moth and rust destroy, and where thieves break in and steal. But store up for yourselves treasures in heaven, where moth and rust do not destroy, and where thieves do not break in and steal. For where your treasure is, there your heart will be also.'* I love the opportunities that God places before us and I think of each of them as a way for us to store up treasures in heaven. This also allows me to live for the higher purpose that my mom always told me about."

Treasures in heaven, what a fascinating concept! What could these treasures be? I can assure you that they are enormously greater than anything from this earthly world. The bible tells us that heaven is a majestic and immensely beautiful place, so treasures in heaven must be breathtaking! Here is how the Apostle John describes the city of Jerusalem coming down out of heaven in *Revelation 21:11*, *"It shone with the glory of God, and it's brilliance was like that of a very precious jewel, like a jasper, clear as crystal"*. John is using the most beautiful things he can think of to describe the holy city. How much more intimate and lovely the treasures in this heavenly city must be. Perhaps the treasures could be more than physical objects, they might also be people we are reunited with in heaven or emotional treasures such as love and joy. Whatever these treasures are, I guarantee that they will be far more precious that anything the human mind can possibly imagine! *1 Corinthians 2:9 says, "No eye has seen, no ear has heard, no mind has conceived what God has prepared for those who love Him"*

Chapter 3

The Greatest Honor Of My Life

The day arrived when I was to do my very first jail ministry visit with just me and the inmates isolated and locked together in a small room deep inside the jail. A few days before, I mentioned to my good friend Angelo that I had to lead ministry service in jail by myself that coming weekend, and that I was a little nervous. "That's because it's game time!" Angelo told me in an excited energetic voice. It was going to be just me by myself, but part of a team with the most astounding mission; to help save souls for all eternity by leading people to a most gracious and loving God and His Son Jesus. I would be leading Sunday Church service to a group of inmates, far inside the jail walls, but of course, I had an invincible God with me! Somehow, I taught that Sunday in jail with an aura of calm confidence. The night before, a flurry of thoughts and emotions were running through my mind, the fear of the unknown. What if I couldn't answer some of the questions about God or the bible and I was not sure if I really wanted to be in a locked room with inmates in a jail. I started to think I would rather be somewhere else (anywhere else). I didn't realize that I had to lead ministry groups by myself. Would I be attacked? Would I just plain rather sleep in and watch a football or basketball game on TV.? It wasn't until a few years into the ministry that I realized that this service was the greatest honor of my life because it was then that I began to comprehend the depth of the majesty, beauty, and holiness of the incredible uncontainable God that I represented each and every time I served in jail. I often share my favorite scripture with the inmates at the beginning of each service. *Isaiah 6:1-5*, from the prophet Isaiah, as he describes a vision he received of mighty God seated on his throne in heaven says. *"In the year King Uzziah died, I saw the Lord seated on a throne, high and exalted, and the train of his robe filled the temple. Above him were Seraphs, each with six wings: With two wings they covered their faces, with two wings they covered their feet, and with two they were flying. And they were calling to one another: 'Holy, holy, holy is the Lord Almighty, the whole earth is full of his glory.' At the sound of their voices the doorposts and thresholds shook and the temple was filled with smoke".* Isaiah was staggered by this vision as he continued and recorded his own reaction, *"Woe to me!" I cried. "I am ruined!" For I am a man of unclean lips and I live among a people of unclean lips, and my eyes have seen the King, the Lord Almighty."* As Isaiah stood in the presence of the absolute splendor and perfection of God, he realized that he was a sinner and it reminds me that if I die today, I will be standing in the presence of a perfect and incomprehensible God. This scripture motivates me to live life differently, not the self-centered life that I used to live and that many are living today. Then I began to reflect on the thought that I serve a God that is so powerful, so majestic, and so holy, even the angels couldn't look directly at Him as He is seated on His throne surrounded by unapproachable light! It's a fascinating and intriguing thought to imagine that the angels could not look directly at the countenance of God! They had to cover their faces with their wings in His presence! This is what drives me and is the source of my passion. The angels were calling out so loudly that the doorposts and thresholds shook. I can't stop thinking about what Isaiah said, *"The earth is full of His Glory"* and I started looking at the world around me differently. I started noticing that God's fingerprints and glory are evident everywhere that I looked, if I would only pause a few moments once in a while and really look at the world around me; The beauty of the blue sky, the peaceful-ness and vast mystery of the oceans, the serenity of a mild wind, the gracefulness of a waterfall or mountain stream, the crystal clear water in the running streams and rivers in Sequoia and Yosemite national parks, the wonderful aroma of pine trees in a forest, and the majesty of the mountain ranges of the Sierra Nevada are just a few examples of the glory and majesty of God. There is not only life on the Earth, but there is a spectacular variety of life! The tropical fish, with their myriad of colors, so many different birds with all kinds of different colors and sizes, even birds that can talk (which is a miracle in itself), the great whales of the ocean, and beautiful dolphins jumping just off the coast of the southern California beaches all testify to His phenomenal majesty. God's glory is also strikingly evident in the vast complexity of the microscopic world as well as we study His creation at the molecular and atomic levels.

A number of years ago, we adopted a rescue dog and named her Mya. Everyone loves to watch her play Frisbee because of her incredible ability to run, jump, and catch a Frisbee in mid-air. I watch her in wonder many times amazed at how God created her to be so athletic. To be able to run and jump with such ease and precision and how beautiful God made her! Mya continues to be highly athletic even as she advances in age. I remember thinking to myself that only God can create something so graceful and magnificent! I have also always been impressed by the cheetah, the fastest land animal in the world. The Cheetah, with its long legs, lean muscle, and thin torso, was designed and created by God to run and hunt and has been clocked running up to 65 miles per hour! Next time you're on the freeway driving at 65mph, look out your side window and imagine a cheetah running next to you as fast as the car! What a graceful and uniquely beautiful animal God has created! The animal world is a vast and glorious display of God's creative ability. The creation of human beings, along with their intellect, emotions, and complexity made in the image of God, is another display of His Glory as He took creation to an even higher level. Most people are so busy and preoccupied with everyday life that they don't take the time to really look around at the astounding beauty of the things that surround them.

I once looked very closely at a tiny flower. The level of detail and vivid colors in the miniature flower petals was remarkable. God put such thought and creativity into the tiniest of flowers and the result is such a thing of beauty. There's an empty, ugly dirt lot that I drive by on my way to jail that I have noticed many times, but one day, after a steady rain, this ugly piece of dirt was filled with colorful wild flowers. I remember thinking to myself how cool it was that God has the ability to change ugly, emptiness into a work of gorgeous art! It was as if this dirt lot was His canvas as He transformed it into a thing of complete beauty. I think that He did the same thing with my life, transforming it from something ugly.

I've also been truly blessed in this life to be able to spend some time in the Hawaiian Islands. The immense beauty of the Islands is truly captivating and is a glorious display of what God can do. On one of my visits, I was walking through a tropical rain forest on the big island of Hawaii and my heart and soul were warmed by God as I walked through the light rain and mist that was in the air surrounded by the lushness of the trees, colorful flowers, and the rich green vegetation. It was as if God Himself was walking with me with His arm around me. The peacefulness was like I have never experienced. I stood in awe and through the mist I watched the water cascade down from a waterfall off in the distance. This was the loveliest

place I have ever seen, and I felt so loved by God that day.
The clear, turquoise-tinted water at the beaches, with its
warmness, is so beautiful to swim in and enjoy. As my wife
Lora and I swam in the ocean one day, a pod of dolphins
swam with us and around us and entertained us by showing
off their exceptional beauty and superior, almost effortless
swimming skills and agility that God gave them! The beauty
and mystery of the volcano and steam vents from the geo-
thermal energy were also on display as we walked around
the island that God created. This is only the beginning of
my discovering His Glory that is so mysteriously, but clearly
displayed as I look at the infinite universe that we live in.
It's as if God is saying, "If you want to know what I am
like, look at the expanse of my exquisite universe that has
no end!" I have a series of photographs that were taken by
cameras (like the Hubble telescope) from satellites that are
cruising through the deep realms of outer space. I bring
them into jail and share them with the inmates as we all
look at them in awe of what our Lord God has created and
see the beautiful celestial bodies and endless, mysterious for-
mations in our universe. Modern day scientists are humbled
as well as baffled as they attempt to understand the images
that our satellites are transmitting back to earth, images of
God's creation that have never been seen before! Our God
not only can create a tiny, beautiful flower, but also created
an unimaginably complex universe that our best scientists
and physicists will never fully understand or comprehend.
Psalm 19:1-4 says, "The heavens declare the glory of God; the

skies proclaim the work of his hands. Day after day they pour forth speech; night after night they display knowledge. There is no speech or language where their voice is not heard. Their voice goes out into all the earth, their words to the ends of the world".

The earth is a tiny planet that sits in the perfect location in our enormous Milky Way Galaxy, a galaxy that can actually be seen from earth on a clear night as you get away from the city lights and look up to the sky. Scientists refer to this place, where the earth sits in our galaxy as the "Goldilox Zone" because it is "just perfect" for life to exist and thrive. It's so incredible that God placed planet earth in the perfect location in the vastness of His infinite universe. I serve an infinite God!

I heard an astronaut describe the beauty of the earth as he viewed it from outer space. He was captivated by the sight of God's beautiful blue planet. He was able to see the earth's atmosphere that he described as the "thin blue line" along the outer circumference of our planet. He was in awe of how unique planet earth is and how it stands out amongst the planets in the billions of galaxies in God's stunning universe. The thin blue line of air that surrounds the earth sustains all of life. I am struck with fascination and wonder every time I see photographs of our universe, with its magnificent beauty. My mind races with thoughts as I try to imagine a God that can create such an infinite and spectacular universe. The bible refers to the universe as the "heavens." What an incredible honor it is to serve an infinitely powerful, merciful and loving God and to be included as one of His own family! The earth is spinning about its own axis at approximately 1,000 miles per hour. The earth is also hurling through space at an unbelievable 67,000 miles per hour, racing through the emptiness of outer space as it continuously orbits the sun year after year throughout all of history. Try to imagine that every year, the earth completes an astonishing 584 million mile trip around the sun as God's son Jesus holds all things in the universe together! *Colossians 1:16-17 says, "…all things were created by Him and for Him. He is before all things, and in Him all things hold together".* Try to imagine the level of power it takes to hold all things together in the universe! Every day on planet earth is a miracle, so don't waste a miracle, do something for God. I guarantee that as you grow old, you will never look back and regret the things you have done for God out of your love for Him. The earth, as well as the life on it, is a brilliant supernatural display of God's magnificent glory. Heaven, the ultimate paradise, can then only be described as so good, that it is incomprehensible to the human mind.

Chapter 4

Some Good News

W hen I speak to the inmates about the Gospel, I first get the group to acknowledge that we are all sinners (including myself) and that our sin separates each one of us from our holy and perfect God forever. I ask for a show of hands, as we read through each one of the 10 commandments together. I ask them to raise their hand if they have broken any of God's commandments. It doesn't take long for them to realize that all of us are hopeless sinners and have broken God's commands thousands of times. Here is the question that I bring forward to the inmates, "How can any of us stand in the throne-room, in the presence of the absolute perfection of our unfathomable Holy God, each one of us admittedly guilty of thousands of sins, and try to explain to Him that we are somehow good people?" The inmates realize that it's kind of ridiculous to think that any of us is a "good person" as compared to the ultimate, flawless, majestic, nature of God. Then comes the Good News! I inform them that God the Father has already fixed this problem by sending his only son Jesus. Jesus is a perfect and eternal being, who also always existed. Jesus willfully stepped down from the perfection of heaven to live a lowly life on earth. Jesus then gave His sinless life to pay the price and absorb the punishment for all of our sins. When Jesus died on the cross for all the sins of mankind, the relationship between sinful man and our Holy God was repaired for those that believe that Jesus is our Savior. The inmates realize the seriousness of the situation as we discuss that Jesus desires that each one of us will also repent, or turn away from, our particular sins. I then give them an illustration to help them understand what Jesus did. I say, "So let's say that a man stands before a judge in court, and the judge tells the man that either he has to pay a $1 million dollar fine, or he has to spend 20 years in prison for his crimes. The man looks down at the ground in despair because he has no money. Then suddenly a good man in the back of the court room stands up and says, 'I will pay the $1 million for him!'. This is similar to what Jesus did for us. He paid the fine for us that we could not pay ourselves, so that we can escape the sentence of eternity in hell, separated from God forever." It turns out that God loves each one of us so deeply, that He offers us every opportunity to believe in our Savior and spend eternity in heaven with Him. Truly a merciful, forgiving, and amazing God filled with love and joy!

Chapter 5

Feeling The Presence Of God

I n jail, we have had shared experiences where some of us have felt the Holy presence of God Himself. God is so far above our human level, that it's hard for me to fathom that He not only allows me to pray to Him, but that He actually hears me and responds to my prayers! Our God that created the universe and breathed the stars of the galaxies from the breath of His mouth! *Psalm 33:6 says, "By the word of the Lord were the heavens made, their starry host by the breath of His mouth."* Typically when I am alone in my truck praying, either on my way to work or to jail for ministry service with the windows rolled up, the radio turned off, and free from outside noise and distractions I have an experience that calms my inner being deep within my soul. As I am praying and thanking God for always loving me and always taking care of me, a feeling of complete peacefulness and calm surrounds and overtakes me. My breathing becomes deep, slow, and even. The ambient temperature in my truck becomes perfect, not too hot or too cold. My body is in a state of complete comfort and relaxation, but I also feel a level of elevated wonder as I am connected directly to the living God! It's amazing that His infinite, uncontainable power comes in the form of tranquil serenity. All of my worries and concerns from this world vanish, and I am overwhelmed with a feeling of complete contentment. I feel a serene warmth in my heart and an intimate closeness to my God. Time ceases for a while, and there is a supernatural connection between me and God. It usually only lasts for a few minutes, but nevertheless, a connection is made and exists between me on the earth and my eternal Father in the far reaches of Heaven. Heaven and earth seem to draw close for a few moments. As I am growing older, I find that I am more aware of God's loving presence around me and my family. I feel that God is going to use me to do something great for His kingdom. I have also experienced similar feelings while at the orphanages in Mexico while interacting with the little children as I watch them run and play, Here, God's presence can last for hours at a time. I have a confident feeling that everything is going to be ok because God is with me and has always been with me, and I know that he will never leave me. Afterwards, my mind runs through my many blessings and how incredible it is that God has extended His spectacular grace to me and my family even though we don't in any way deserve it. I marvel at His rich mercy, grace, and love. I began to understand why Jesus often retreated alone to pray as explained in *Luke 5:16, "But Jesus often withdrew to lonely places and prayed" and Matthew 14:23, "After He had dismissed them, He went up on a mountainside by himself to pray."*

Some of the inmates have shared different kinds of experiences where God has given them a specific message about something very urgent and current in their lives. One inmate was facing a possible long-term 20-year sentence. He was very distraught and decided to pray and cry out passionately to God. A guard came to his cell one day and pulled him out for a meeting. As he was walking down the jail corridor, he was certain that very bad news was coming. He sat down in the meeting, and to his amazement he was told that a new program was just put in place and that he would be freed on probation in 6 months. He felt that God told him, "I'm giving you another chance". My advice to him was simple, "God has graciously given you a second chance. Don't blow it! Use your life for good in Gods name" The inmate is now a true believer in the power of prayer!

Chapter 6

The Wonderful Gift Of Freedom

One of the common themes I've encountered in the inmate's prayer requests is a longing to be with their families. The inmates have lost their freedom, and sometimes we humans don't appreciate things until we lose them. Freedom is truly a magnificent gift, and each one of us decides how we use this precious gift from God. Over the years, as I listened to the prisoners talk about how much they miss their families, it would make me think about my own family. After I finished ministry service, I would excitedly drive home, so I could hug my children and embrace my wife and tell all of them how much I love them. God has given me an unimaginable gift of complete freedom. Dennis Philpot, my mentor, friend, and fellow jail minister explains it like this. "Thirty-one years ago, when leaving jail one day, I looked at the inmates as I walked out. Some had bullet wounds, and some had scars. I thought to myself, these people have lost their friends, lost their marriages, lost their jobs, lost what relationships they had with their children, and to top it all off, lost the only thing they had left, their freedom. They have literally lost everything." Dennis explained further, "I count my blessings every day, and I have a new perspective when I hear people complaining about everyday kinds of things. In some places in the world, people are thrown in jail just for being a Christian." Dennis helped me see freedom with a little more insight. As for myself, when I walk out of jail after Sunday ministry, I am so deeply grateful for my freedom. I can see the mountains and fields of fruit trees from the parking lot, and I notice that the sky looks a little more blue, and the breeze feels a little fresher because of my freedom. I sometimes stop and get a cup of coffee on my way home. It tastes better on those days. My God has given me this gift and allows me to live in the freest country in the world! I also realized that God will always be sovereign King with or without me, but He gives me, an ordinary person, an opportunity to be His spokesperson, His child, and He provides an open door for me to actively participate in His plan for eternity and humanity. I am living proof that God will use anyone. You only need to have a heart to serve the Lord for His kingdom. *2 Corinthians 3:17 "Now the Lord is the Spirit, and where the Spirit of the Lord is, there is freedom."* As we follow the Holy Spirit, we begin to gain freedom from the weight of our sins. This is very refreshing and invigorating and it takes a huge load off our shoulders. Life on earth, with its struggles and challenges, is hard enough without having to sling a large burden of sin around with us every day. The Lord's Holy Spirit brings freedom if we follow His gentle guidance. It is crucial that I never forget to thank God for this gift of freedom. Jesus is the one who gave up His freedom, and His precious supernatural life as a ransom to purchase freedom from eternal punishment for all those who believe in His name. *1 Timothy 2:5-6 says, "…the man Christ Jesus, who gave himself as a ransom for all men.."* What Jesus did was colossal because of who He is. If one human being gives up his life for another human being, then that person will be remembered as a hero, but Jesus's life was different because He is God's only Son, a holy and perfect being. His life is of immeasurable and immense value, a sinless, beautiful, holy, and supernatural life was freely given to save all of mankind! This makes Jesus the highest level of hero that is nearly unfathomable. The sacrifice and suffering of Jesus was predicted by the prophet Isaiah in 740bc (740 years before Jesus was born) in *Isaiah 52:14, "Just as there were many who were appalled at him. His appearance was so disfigured beyond that of any man and his form marred beyond human likeness"* Isaiah 53:5 *"But He was pierced for our transgressions, He was crushed for our iniquities; the punishment that brought us peace was upon him, and by his wounds we are healed."* It's hard to read the words of Isaiah without feeling deep sadness in my heart for the suffering that my humble but magnificent Savior endured for us. God the Father gave up His innocent Son, and Jesus in turn, freely gave up His own life to save sinners like me! Believe me, I don't deserve it. If a person claims to believe in His name, then that person's daily actions should reflect his or her faith. Our actions (or good works) do not, in themselves, save us, but instead are a byproduct of our faith. Even though we are made in the image of God, the following scripture demonstrates that God is magnitudes above our human level. *Revelation 4:2-6 says, "At once I was in the Spirit, and there before me was a throne in heaven with someone sitting on it. And the one who sat there had the appearance of jasper and carnelian. A rainbow, resembling an emerald, encircled the throne. Surrounding the throne were twenty four other thrones, and seated on them were twenty four elders. They were dressed in white and had crowns of gold on their heads. From the throne came flashes of lightning, rumblings and peals of thunder".* It's a frightening thought to try to imagine the level of power released when Jesus was murdered! This miraculous supernatural power brings freedom to all of mankind, to those who believe in His name. Matthew describes what happened at the moment that Jesus died on the cross in *Matthew 27:51 says, "At that moment the curtain in the temple was torn in two from top to bottom. The earth shook and the rocks split. The tombs broke open and the bodies of many holy people who had died were raised to life. They came out of the tombs, and after Jesus resurrection, they went into the holy city and appeared to many people."* Jesus defeated death and Satan himself by his death on the cross.

I live in Southern California and have experienced two major earthquakes, one in 1971 and a much larger one in 1994. The power released during an earthquake is utterly tremendous. The earthquake that occurred at the moment that Jesus died on the cross was so massive and powerful that it split rocks. This is difficult to imagine, but this gives us a glimpse of the power of God! This is the power that was released when the innocent and supernatural life of His Son was brutally taken from Him, the power that freed us from the slavery of sin and fixed the relationship between man and God. There is much more at stake here than our earthly freedom. Our freedom for all eternity is on the line. If we refuse to believe in God and His son we will not follow His commands, any hope for eternal freedom is lost in the prisons of hell. However, if we do believe in God and His son we will follow His commands and the eternal freedoms in heaven are given to us as an unimaginable gift from God our Father.

Chapter 7

Jail, A Reason And Safe Place For Some

The first time an inmate told me that he felt safe in jail, I was taken back a little. He told me that he was afraid of getting out of jail and going back to the streets. "Why are you afraid of getting out?" I inquired. "Because I am away from drugs in here," he said. It turned out that he was so addicted to drugs, that the only safe place for him was jail. He told me that his addiction was so powerful that when he thought about drugs, he could actually taste them in his mouth. He also felt safe since the jail enforces strict rules and regulations. I think God uses jail to allow certain people a safe place to evaluate themselves and their lives in a sober condition away from the rest of the world. I see inmates walking down the corridors in jail clutching their bibles tightly. Even the most violent criminals realize the power and wisdom contained in the book from God, the only book that is filled with direct communication from our Creator. The world we live in today is also very afraid of the bible and there is a movement going on to try to remove Christianity and its beliefs from this earth (Lawrence Sellin 10-14-16'... the political genocide of Christianity'). I became aware that I shared something in common with every prisoner. Our faith in our Creator is the powerful common bond that we all share. This allowed me, as an outsider, to communicate with inmates that I would otherwise have nothing in common with. Their world of drugs, alcohol, violence, and crime was so alien to me, yet I could walk into a jail, into a room filled with total strangers, and we could talk together as brothers because of the power and warmth of God's word. *Mark 3:35 says, "Whoever does God's will, is my brother and sister and mother."* I many times experienced an unexplainable passion in my heart in the small detaining rooms amongst the inmates. God finds broken people in jail and turns them back to Himself. It's truly gratifying to see His supernatural power at work in the jail. The inmates also have something that the rest of the world is longing for. They have plenty of time. Jail is a safe place for them to spend time alone with God. I also feel a sense of safeness when I am in jail. The inmates and I can openly and freely talk about God and His word with no outside distractions or hatred from the outside world.

In the world outside of jail, it seems that many of the inmate's problems stemmed from homelessness. Being homeless easily leads to drinking alcohol and taking drugs. The alcohol and drug lifestyle eventually leads back to jail. Many are trapped in this cycle, but there is an answer. There is infinite wisdom from God and His words of beauty. The Bible has the answers and solutions to all of life directly from our Creator. Each person needs to seek out and find this for themselves. You see, the passages in the Bible define a completely new lifestyle that is centered around loving and caring for God and others, not our selfish interests.

Another important aspect of jail is that God may be placing certain people in there for a reason as part of His ultimate plan. The apostle Paul used his time in prison to proclaim and advance the Gospel and to preach to the guards. Paul's authenticity was attractive and fascinating to many people who heard him speak while in prison. *Philippians 1:12-13 says, "Now I want you to know brothers, that what has happened to me has really served to advance the gospel. As a result, it has become clear throughout the whole palace guard and to everyone else that I am in chains for Christ. Because of my chains, most brothers in the Lord have been encouraged to speak the word of God more courageously and fearlessly."* it is truly amazing that Paul, through the power of God, was able to motivate and encourage many people by his actions and spoken words while confined and shackled in prison! When I'm in jail, I discuss this very point with the inmates by telling them that they themselves can reach others deeper within the jail walls where I don't have access. This may be the very reason that God placed them there, to reach and save people from hopeless despair, to reach the unreachable. So, you see how God sets up a network of His people to effectively spread His word. The Holy Spirit along with my church, Bible, and Christian radio bring the messages to me. I bring the messages and Gospel to the inmates who come out for Sunday church service and the inmates, in turn, bring God's word deeper within the jail where only they can reach. Some inmates may be relocated to other jails or prisons and God's word continues to spread. Some of the inmates are even known in jail to be like pastors to others who are hungry for God's word. Some of them have expressed to me their desire to become real ordained pastors when they get out of jail. This chain of people forms a lifeline between us and our God, an eternal lifeline that can't be broken by anyone.

Chapter 8

Led By The Holy Spirit

S ometimes as I sat there in jail, I wondered, "How did I ever get here in the first place? What circumstances and decisions brought me here?" I spent a lot of time thinking about my questions, thinking and reading the Bible. Then it occurred to me, " Was I was led here by the Holy Spirit, the Spirit of God himself?" This concept of being "led by the Spirit" is mentioned in the Bible, a book inspired by God and written thousands of years ago. I thought that only one of God's holy prophets or maybe only God's Son Himself could experience something like this. Could this exact thing have been happening to me in the year 2022? Then I read *Romans 8:9-11 which says "You, however, are controlled not by the sinful nature but by the Spirit, if the Spirit of God lives in you. And if anyone does not have the Spirit of Christ, he does not belong to Christ. But if Christ is in you, your body is dead because of sin, yet your spirit is alive because of righteousness. And if the Spirit of Him, who raises Christ from the dead is living in you, He who raised Christ from the dead will also give life to your mortal bodies through his Spirit, who lives in you."* Personally, I'm convinced that nothing else could have brought me to serve in jail and to help the homeless and others in need. The Holy Spirit of God is the only reason that I'm able to have the courage and strength to do these things. Performing these types of things out of love for God makes our existence complete. The Holy Spirit of God enables us to do things that are impossible to do by ourselves. *Philippians 4:13 says, "I can do everything through him who gives me strength."* God's Holy Spirit draws us out of our comfort zones and gives us a new confidence to try and experience new things, things of God. The other benefit of being led by the Holy Spirit is that He accompanies us and is with us helping in our particular ministries and struggles. Many times, I walk into jail not knowing exactly what I will say that day, but God's Spirit always shows up, and I have never been at a loss for words for one to two hours at a time. Never underestimate the supreme power of God's Holy Spirit. The Holy Spirit of God also enables us to experience things, such as love and joy, at a much higher spiritual level. For example, I am able to love my wife and children at a very high supernatural level, much beyond that of any ordinary non-believing person, due to the Holy Spirit of God that lives in me. The Holy Spirit is our Helper at all times, particularly when we are struggling or weak. *2 Corinthians 12:9-10 says, "…My grace is sufficient for you, for my power is made perfect in weakness….For when I am weak, then I am strong."* God's Spirit empowers us to get through those difficult times in life that tend to occur on nearly a daily basis. The Holy Spirit of God also enables us to feel compassion for our fellow men or women, which includes those that are in jail or those that are homeless without hope. The Word of God often brings warmth, peace, and promise into the dark world of the prisoners and to the homeless on the street. In the Bible, Jesus himself was led by the Holy Spirit when He was fasting and tempted by Satan in the desert. It's hard for me to describe how wonderful and deeply fulfilling it is to be led by the Holy Spirit of God. It's an energy that spreads throughout my being and radiates outward for the world to see God's glory. *John 15:5 says, "I am the vine; you are the branches. If a man remains in me and I in him, he will bear much fruit; apart from me you can do nothing."* None of us can do anything apart from Jesus, and if we are led by God's Spirit, then we are His sons and daughters. *Romans 8:14 says, "because those that are led by the Spirit of God are sons of God"* There is no greater status a human can attain then to become a son or daughter of an incomprehensible God! The Holy Spirit of God has also given me new confidence that I can defeat Satan at any time that I choose. I don't have to live in fear of Satan or his demons due to the inner strength I have from God's Spirit. It's a very special gift from God to those that love Him and respect and follow His commands. We become one of the super warriors in God's army when we are led by His Spirit. The Holy Spirit also elevates our inner strength and courage to new spiritual heights. *2 Timothy 1:7 says, "For God did not give us a spirit of timidity, but a spirit of power, of love, and of self discipline"* I have seen these attributes mentioned by Timothy become sharpened inside of me through my journey in jail ministry. The self discipline of being prepared, of getting up early and serving in the honor of God and being able to teach with power and authority in His name are all things I have experienced ministering in jail. Sometimes I wake up very tired and think about staying in bed, but something overcomes me and gets me up and out of bed when I have committed to serve. I think about the inmates that have been longing for Sunday church service all week and this motivates me to get my rear end out of bed and get going. God needs me to get up and get to work! I am a soldier in the army of the almighty God! What a magnificent position of honor God has bestowed on me!

Chapter 9

God's Call Brings Adventure

I have always enjoyed adventure books and movies, and God gives each of us spiritual gifts that He wants us to use in our daily lives. *Romans 12:6 says, "We have different gifts, according to the grace given us."* It's a fascinating concept to combine the two. How about real adventure combined with using our spiritual gifts? And how about living the adventure instead of watching it or reading about it? This is what God wants for each of us, to live it. Since we all have unique gifts from the Holy Spirit, we need to use these gifts in our every day lives. Don't waste your life playing it safe sitting on the couch watching TV or excessively drinking alcohol. I sometimes use a football analogy for this. If we aren't using and developing our spiritual gifts, we are like a football player on a Superbowl team that just sits on the bench and never plays in the game. Do we want to play in the championship game, or do we want to sit around and watch from the sidelines like any ordinary spectator? The call from God is so far above any Superbowl or any sports game. God calls us to help other people, spread His word to every far corner of the earth, to go into jails and prisons,

39

to help the homeless on the street, and to help orphans and widows. We are called to take personal risks for God. The message of the Bible is not to play it safe, but to risk everything for God's purposes. The apostle Paul describes his life for Jesus in *2 Corinthians 11:25 when he says, "Three times I was beaten with rods, once I was stoned, three times I was shipwrecked, I spent a night and day on the open sea, I have been constantly on the move, I have been in danger from rivers, in danger from bandits, in danger from my own countrymen, in danger from Gentiles, in danger in the city, in danger in the country, in danger at sea, and in danger from false brothers. I have labored and toiled and have often gone without sleep; I have known hunger and thirst, and have often gone without food; I have been cold and naked. Besides everything else, I face daily pressure of my concern for all the churches."* Does it sound like Paul had a boring life? Going into jail has it risks, but it also has rich adventure, rewards, and fulfillment. I never know what's going to happen on any particular day during jail ministry, but that sense of adventure is always present. I know that if each of us listens to God's call and makes sacrifices in our lives for His work, I guarantee you will never live a boring life. I never know what to expect each time I walk into jail, but I've seen powerful effects on people's lives take place over and over. On Sunday, I grab my Bible and study notes, a cup of coffee, and I drive towards the jail not knowing what each day in jail may do to my life or the inmates' lives. On my way to jail, I marvel over the wonder and beauty of God's creation as I see the green rolling hills and small farms along the way. I get to hear many testimonies from the inmates about how God has shown up in their lives and helped them when circumstances looked very bad. One inmate told me that he was hanging out with his neighborhood crowd one night in the front yard, and they saw a police car coming towards them. They all scattered and ran in different directions thinking that the police were going to arrest them. This particular inmate ran and ran until he was very far away from the police. In fact, he had run so far, that he was now in enemy gang territory at night by himself. He decided to get out of there as fast as possible, but it wasn't long before the rival gang found him. "You're in the wrong neighborhood," they said to him. "Get on your knees". He knelt down on the sidewalk in the dark. The gang member proceeded to pull out a gun and put it to his head as he knelt on the sidewalk. The inmate closed his eyes thinking, "I guess this is the end. Here I am at night all by myself. I will never see my friends or family ever again." Then suddenly, for no apparent reason, the man pulled the gun away and let him go. The inmate ran a little and in desperation, knocked on a stranger's door. An older woman answered. "Can I use your phone to call a friend?" He inquired. The woman said, "You're in trouble aren't you?" "Yes," he answered. Then the woman said something that the inmate will never forget to this day. She said, "I'll let you use my phone under one condition". The inmate said, "What condition is that?" She said, "If you promise to go to church with me this coming Sunday, you can use my phone." He was blown away that she would allow an apparent gang banger trouble-maker and stranger to come into her home, use her phone, and then invite him to church! "It was a miracle that God let me live that night," he recalled, "and this woman let me use her phone if I promised to go to church with her". "Wow", he said "God showed up that night." He ended up taking the woman up on her offer. She picked him up for church that next Sunday. God showed this man what grace and mercy looked like, first sparing his life, and then immediately opening a door to get him back to church. All of us who attended that particular Sunday for jail ministry, felt the inmate's near-death encounter as he almost lost his life, but instead, was given a second chance as he was called back to God and back to church. We follow a God of second chances. Sometimes God's wake-up calls are pretty blatant, whatever it takes to get our attention. The more stubborn we are, the more blunt God can be sometimes. My Christian brother Frank shared his testimony with me. "My marriage and life were a mess when I was younger," Frank told me. "I was drinking, doing a lot of drugs, treating my wife like garbage, and basically being a first class knuckle head. I was working in a trench at my construction job one day when a skip-loader full of cement blocks was moving overhead and a concrete block fell on me with enough impact to crack my hard hat and also my scull. They told me in the hospital that I probably wouldn't live, but by some miracle, I survived. After surviving that, God turned my life around and I became a

Christian. I started treating my wife and children with the love that God intended. Can you imagine that God got my attention by dropping a block of concrete on my head?" God will get our attention in a clear and forceful fashion if we ignore His calling.

Chapter 10

A Sense Of Urgency

As I'm growing older, I find myself feeling a greater sense of urgency towards the matters of God and my calling to do His work. As each day goes by, I have less time left on Earth, and I am one day closer to seeing God in His holy throne room. I'm not worthy of standing in His presence, but because of his Son's death, it changed everything. *2 Corinthians 5:21 says, "God made him who had no sin to be sin for us, so that in Him we might become the righteousness of God."* None of us will live in our mortal, aging, earthly bodies forever, and nobody knows exactly how much time each one of us has left on earth. We all need to use our time wisely and be deliberate about expressing our faith in daily actions until they become natural for us. The prisoners have also shared with me their feeling of urgency in turning their lives around. Many of them are stuck in a cycle of going in and out of jail. The best hope of getting out of jail and living a fulfilling life rests in God alone and His Word. God has planted a desire in their hearts to draw them nearer to Him. Jesus said it so simply, "*Love God and love your neighbor*". It's unbelievable that Jesus could summarize the entire Bible with six words. It's also a testament to His incredible genius. It sounds easy, but sometimes it's not that easy to live this out. I explain to the inmates how to get started. There is a scripture that is my favorite for this topic because it's so simple, straightforward, and practical. *Galatians 5:22-23 says, "But the fruit of the Spirit is love, joy, peace, patience, kindness, goodness, faithfulness, gentleness, and self-control. Against such things there is no law".* The fruit of the Spirit is beautifully and elegantly stated and reminds us to follow these simple guidelines of deep and great wisdom. The fruit of the Spirit is so practical that we can implement them in our daily lives. Pick a fruit of the Spirit for Monday. Say we choose "love" for Monday. We must be very deliberate as we plan our day. I will practice "love" on Monday. I will display love to my wife and children, to my coworkers, to strangers that I may encounter during the day and yes, even to my enemies. It feels deeply gratifying to really do these kinds of things in our everyday lives. Wouldn't it be nice to lift up and encourage our spouse instead of being overly critical and tearing them down frequently? On Tuesday, I will practice "joy". I will be joyful on Tuesday no matter what life throws at me. If you are a joyful person, people like being around you, people are attracted to a joyful life, and this provides opportunity for sharing our faith. I have noticed that younger people sometimes like spending time with my wife Lora and I and I think that they are somewhat intrigued by our joyful life and the blessed partnership through marriage that God has graciously given to Lora and myself for so many years. On Wednesday, I will practice "peace". We can display peace amongst this crazy pace of life by not over-reacting or getting angry over simple situations like waiting in line or being stuck in traffic or something simple that's going wrong around the house. Things happen in life, and our day rarely goes as we planned it. We can also become the peace-makers when conflict grows around us. On Thursday, I will display "patience". We can display patience by letting others speak first and by being good listeners instead of talking too much. Be patient and compassionate to other people and this will honor God. We can be patient with our children as well. On Friday, I will practice "kindness". As Christians, we can really stand out by displaying kindness in this cold world. This can simply be sharing our resources with others or speaking to people with kind and appreciative words. On Saturday, I will show "goodness" to the people that I come in contact with. Being good to others can be as easy as giving our time to our fellow man that may be in need of a friend to lean on or someone to talk to. *Ephesians 2:10 (From NLT study bible) says, "For we are God's masterpiece. He has created us anew in Christ Jesus, so we can do good things that he planned for us long ago"* This one stopped me in my tracks! So, if we believe that Jesus is our Savior, we will follow God's Spirit and we are transformed from enemies of God into one of His masterpieces! This is a mind-boggling concept, to be a masterpiece of the majestic living God! I noticed in the Bible that Jesus was never too busy and always made time to stop and talk to others. Then He truly cared about the person He was talking to and helped them with great compassion. Jesus always made time to talk to those who were in trouble, and if we think we're busy, imagine how busy Jesus was on His mission to save the entire world, all of mankind! Some of my friends from elementary school, as well as some of my former coworkers, have already passed away from this life. Each time this happens, it makes me stop and think about the brevity of our lives on earth, and I reflect on how I can improve myself with the time I have left. On Sunday, I will display faithfulness to God by putting Him first and trusting in Him for all aspects of my life. If God chooses to end my life soon (maybe today), I need to make sure that I'm living in faith, and that my daily actions are going hand-in-hand with my faith. The next day I will work on gentleness, starting with my wife and then extending it to others throughout the day. And then finally I will exhibit self-control. One aspect of self-control is saying no to those things that do not honor God. This is how we discuss self-control in jail. Let's take an inmate that struggles with alcohol addiction. Maybe he serves his sentence and gets released from jail. He goes back to his old neighborhood, and his old friends are happy to see him, so they throw him a welcome home party. Music is playing and everyone is drinking, and they slide a bottle of tequila and a shot glass in front of him. "Time to party and get drunk," his homey yells out." "Not today," the ex-inmate says" "Why not, you're out of jail," homey retorts. "I became a Christian in jail," he says,

"I don't drink anymore." Everyone at the party is stunned and bewildered. How can he just stop drinking like that? As the ex-inmate displays self-control, his decisions now bring glory to God, not himself. We can all bring glory to God by demonstrating self-control to those around us. The fruit of the spirit is extremely powerful when a person actually lives it out in his or her life. I find the words in Galatians 5 to be extremely wise yet so simple and very refreshing. One person, practicing the fruit of the Spirit, can make a huge difference in this crazy world. Just imagine the impact if we all practiced it daily! Each one of us can be a true light and beacon to the world by living out the fruit. *Matthew says, 5:14-16 "You are the light of the world. A city on a hilltop cannot be hidden. Neither do people light a lamp and put it under a bowl. Instead they put it on a stand, and it gives light to everyone in the house. In the same way, let your light shine before men, that they may see your good deeds and praise your Father in heaven."* Many times God uses broken lives and turns them around for His glory. I want to use my life to bring glory to God, not to myself. I always tell the prisoners that I am not spreading God's word in jail because I'm some kind of great person, but instead, I give full credit and glory to God for pulling me out of my worldly self-centered mundane life and allowing me to become part of His life! God has given me so many wonderful blessings that I can't count them all. A blessing from God is very personal and deeply touching for me. I think about God's greatness and un-tethered supreme power and the fact that He notices me and listens to my prayers and sees my actions, that's so incredible to me. God notices me and blesses me! He sees me and pours His great grace and mercy on me! I can just simply say that I don't deserve His blessings because of my sinful messed up life, but He continues to pour His blessings on me! How can I not love a God like this? I continue to warmly learn about Him, I want to seek Him always and make my life count for something. I don't want to just be another loser on this planet, wasting my life away for nothing. I've had this discussion many times with the inmates about not wasting their lives! Our human lives are extremely precious because of the supernatural blood that was spilled to save us. Remember that each one of us has the potential to become one of God's masterpieces by Him that created an infinite universe that includes everything that lives and breathes! I want everyone to walk with God and to experience the deep satisfaction and sense of wonder and joy that comes from truly knowing Him and receiving His glorious blessings. I pray that all of us can experience and live a life deeply filled with God's rich and loving grace.

Chapter 11

Does God Really Care About Me And What I Am Doing In Jail?

There have been those times, however, when I wonder if God sees what I am doing in jail or even cares. I have asked myself, "Am I doing the right things to please God?" God has a lot going on and is busy running a universe and I am just one little person among the billions of people on this planet. Mankind has also asked this question throughout the centuries. *Psalm 144:3 says, "O Lord, what is man that you care for him, the son of man that you think of him?"* But the truth is that God cares very deeply! When I wonder if I could give up one of my children's lives for someone else, it is an unthinkable act to me, but that's exactly what God did with His Son Jesus. God cares about us so intimately, that He freely gave His Son's life for all of us. The life of Jesus has to be the most precious possession that God could give up, but He loves us with deep supernatural passionate love, not the superficial love that mankind typically exhibits. *Romans 8:38-39 says, "For I am convinced that neither death nor life, neither angels nor demons, neither the present nor the future, nor any powers, neither height nor depth, nor anything else in creation, will be able to separate us from the love of God that is in Christ Jesus our Lord."*

There was one inmate that I spoke to that was so ashamed of what he had done in the past, that he now has trouble looking people in the eye. He looked down at the ground when he spoke to me. "At least you are doing good in your life," he said, "teaching Gods word in jail." I told him to remember that we are all sinners (including me) and we all fall short of God's glorious standards, but that doesn't mean that any of us should be ashamed forever by what we have done. God, through his son Jesus, cleans our slate and allows us to move forward with strength, righteousness, and courage no matter what we have done in the past as long as we confess and repent from our sins and ask Him for forgiveness. *Philippians 3:9 says, "And be found in him, not having a righteousness of my own that comes from the law, but that which is through faith in Christ – the righteousness that comes from God and is by faith."* We can become righteous in God's eyes by believing in our hearts that His Son Jesus paid the penalty for our sins by His suffering and death on the cross. This changes everything since we would otherwise be eternally separated from God because of our sins. One of the other wondrous attributes of God is that He can make things new again. In my own life, God has rescued me and given me a new beginning many times when I was in the deepest despair. *Psalm 118:5-6 says, "In my anguish I cried to the Lord, and He answered by setting me free."* When I read this verse, I first paused, and then felt a warm sense of joy pour over me and through my soul. Was God talking directly to me? I know that He was because He had recently set me free from a very difficult and stressful job situation by giving me a new job, a new beginning. The Lord of the universe and all eternity heard the prayers of one little person on earth and set me free! I now openly proclaim (and will continue) to those in jail and anyone else that our God does intimately care about each and every one of us. I'm feeling a deep sense of love as I am writing these words. There have been instances in my life where I felt that God was holding my hand and helping me get through this difficult life and this was one of them.

After my career in Aerospace, I became a manager and consultant for a construction company, and after prayer, I have seen our work-crew accomplish things that are impossible without direct miracles from God! I can now confidently tell the prisoners that God will set those free who ask for His help. Why try to solve all of life's problems on our own when we have such a powerful and loving Father that is eager to help us if we just ask Him in prayer? Pray often and pray with passion, and then see God do His work!

Chapter 12

Living For God And His Son, We Are Of Great Value

We can all choose to live our lives in one of two ways, with value or without value. Jesus Himself lived a life of tremendous value and at the highest level because He lived according to God's will. He lived and died serving others, not Himself. Jesus is the perfect model of how to live our lives. He lived a humble life without a lot of money or possessions or political power, yet He was able to impact the world like no other person in history. In fact, Jesus was homeless during the last 3 years of His ministry. Jesus showed us how to live life at an optimum and peak level without physical possessions. We discuss in jail that God created each of us to do good works, make disciples of other men, and bring Glory to His name. I know this isn't easy to do in this modern age and in our everyday lives, that's why we have the Holy Spirit Himself living inside of us and helping us every day. It's funny how the modern world tells us that living life to the fullest has to involve drinking beer and going to parties. God's way of living life to its fullest is so much more. As I mentioned before, it involves giving, not receiving. *Acts 20:35 says, "…It is more blessed to give than to receive".* I have never experienced a deeper sense of warmth and purpose than when I give to others. It's something that I can't describe. You have to experience it for yourself. The feeling of handing food to a hungry child, or giving a pair of shoes to someone who can't afford to buy them, there is nothing else like it. It kind of stuns your heart, in a good way. It's a lasting feeling of well-being and closeness to other people and to our Creator. How refreshing is it to know that we serve a God of love. *1 John 4:8 says, "Whoever does not love does not know God because God is love."* Love is an extremely powerful emotion that we received from our heavenly Father since we are all created in His image. Love goes far beyond this earthly world. I still feel love for people that were in my life, but have passed away, like my father. My father passed away about 14 years ago, but I still love him. This is a strong illustration for me of love going beyond our immediate physical world into eternity. It wouldn't make sense for us to love someone who has passed away unless there is a hope of an eternal existence where we can be with them again. God offers us eternal life, full of joy, and completely free of pain and suffering. God must feel that each one of us is very valuable to offer us such a great and precious gift! I frequently plead with the inmates to make each one of their lives count for something. Using our lives for God's purposes is the key to this life and to an everlasting life full of joy.

Chapter 13

<u>Children's Prison In Mexico</u>

In Fall of 2017, I had the privilege of interviewing Pastor Von about his 15 years of ministry in children's prison in Mexico. He described the prison as about 300 to 400 teens and pre-teens, the youngest being about ten years old. "Some of them had already murdered," he said, "murdered with no remorse. The younger children seemed proud of the fact that they had murdered someone because they thought it made them appear like some kind of tough guy to their peers." Pastor Von is approaching 90 years old these days, but he has been working not only in the children's prison but has been helping the poor and also the fatherless children in Mexico for many years. Pastor Von told me "The first time I went in the prison, I had my Bible, and I was wearing nice clothes. That got me the middle finger," he laughed, "I guess I needed to change my approach." He continued, "I went back with some shrunken skulls that I picked up in the Amazon and also chocolate candy bars. I became quite popular with my new approach". He noted that he was always accompanied by a translator. "My translator was Julian. It humbled me because I needed Julian to do the Lord's work in Mexico because of the language barrier. I couldn't do it alone. I used to wash the boy's feet in prison, and the boys would ask me why I did that. My answer was, because I love you and care about you and also because that's what the Lord Himself would have done". *John 13:4-5 says, "...so He got up from the meal, took off his outer clothing, and wrapped a towel around his waist. After that, He poured water into a basin and began to wash His disciple's feet, drying them with the towel that was wrapped around him."* The significance of what Jesus did is massive. Try to comprehend that the Creator of the Universe, who has always existed, who holds the power of all that has been created, the Commander of an invincible army of Angels, a God that created the stars of our universe by the breath from His mouth, would perform a common servant's act of humility by washing someone's feet! Our Lord and Savior humbled and lowered himself to a slave-level to show us how to be humble. Pastor Von has given his life to the Lord, and I have met very few people in this world who have actually done this. Pastor Von explained, "Coming from a strict German background, it doesn't come naturally for me to hug people and show affection to others, but God has enabled me to break through these barriers. Once we understand what Jesus did for us on the cross, we can then start to understand grace and our need for the Holy Spirit. Being a conservative Baptist, I thought that doing God's work would take away all the fun in life, but instead, God amplified my life and made His work an adventure". Pastor

Von has carried God's word deep into the jungles of the Amazon as part of his walk with God as well, a little more fun than sitting around on the couch and watching TV. I asked him if he had become closer to God through his ministry work. "Yes, I have," he explained, "I have also gained more insights and God has helped me to be able to speak to people and has given me the ability to explain things to others". I'm deeply encouraged by Pastor Von's life as a servant of God, and I have had the privilege of ministering to the poor side-by-side in Mexico with him and his ministry team. The first time I participated with Pastor Von's ministry team, I was stunned by what I saw and experienced. I fully experienced the love of God that day as we gave the children baths and supplied food and clothing to the poor families in Mexico. God has helped me realize the empty shallowness of living the self-centered life that many Americans live today, as contrasted to the infinitely rich life that He has intended for us to live before the creation of mankind, a life that has the potential to bring glory to the name of the Lord. *Ephesians 1:4 says, "For He chose us in Him before the creation of the world".*

I want to share something that happened to me one day when I was serving the poor in Mexico with Pastor Von. It's hard to have a one-on-one conversation with him due to all the people and swirl of busyness around him just prior to crossing the border into Mexico with his team. I prayed to God in the days before one of the trips that I would somehow be able to speak to him privately. The day of the trip came, and I drove to San Diego to meet with Pastor Von and his ministry team. Everything went as usual, packing the vans with food, clothing, toys, medicine, and drinks for the children and families. Just as we were about to depart, Pastor Von said in a loud voice, "I have room for one person in my car. Would anyone like to ride with me?" I raised my hand, "I'll ride with you," I said. I jumped into Pastor Von's car and what happened in the next 60 minutes or so, changed my life forever. "Do you mind if we stop for coffee?" he asked. "No, I love coffee and I would like to pay for yours, anything you want," I replied. "Ok, but I like the expensive stuff," he laughed. As we drove and stopped and drank coffee, I told him that I was very impressed with his ministry and it really touched me to be part of this wonderful work he was doing for God. Pastor Von was very humble and wanted no credit or praise for all the years of work and the thousands of little children and their families that he has helped. As we crossed the border into Mexico he said, "Do you mind if we make one more stop along the way?" "I don't mind at all," I said. He commented, "It's someone's birthday and I want to drop off a gift at the children's home." He explained that he had opened a home in Mexico many years ago to help the fatherless children get off the streets and have a safe place to live. As we approached the orphanage home, Pastor Von slowed his car down as the children came running down the street towards us. They began to jump on his car and hang onto the side as we slowly drove down the street. This reminded me of when the little children came to Jesus in the Bible. You see, they knew his car because Pastor Von was their father. God gave these fatherless children in Mexico an earthly father that loved them. I had never seen anything like it. The connection that he had with the children was so innocent and pure. What I experienced that day was the feeling of the full and unfiltered love of God. As I spent time that day in a third world country, seeing the love of God with my own eyes, hearing the voices of the children, and walking around the orphanage, I remember thinking that our lives and problems in the United States seemed so silly and insignificant at times. What I saw in Mexico was much more serious, real life and death struggles. I now understand why a person like Pastor Von would live his life this way. He gets to feel the way I did, but feel it every day of his life, not just once in a while like I did. He has lived his life to the fullest, and I understand that's what God wants for us. I think it's the closeness to God that I crave and long for, and its right there in front of me and in front of all of us, if we just reach out and grab a hold of it.

Chapter 14

Why Does Jesus Call Us To Visit The Prisoners?:

Imagine being locked in a jail cell for 20 hours per day, isolated from your family and friends, only allowed to come out of your cell for 4 hours each day within the jail confinement walls. That's the reality that many of the inmates are facing. Sometimes the only difference between ourselves and the inmates is that they got caught and we didn't. Jesus understood there may be some in jail or prison that might actually be innocent. The inmates have told me that they greatly look forward to the Sunday jail ministry time and the comfort and encouragement they receive from God's word. I can't imagine what it would be like if nobody came to visit me if I were in jail. The loneliness in and of itself is enough to kill a person. In the Bible, the list of people who served jail time has some pretty big names on it: Joseph, Jeremiah, John the Baptist, Apostle Peter, Apostle Paul, Apostle John, and Jesus himself who was arrested and falsely sentenced to death. This is actually a list of innocent people that were arrested or thrown into prison. Jesus experienced the feeling of devastating betrayal as His apostles abandoned Him. Hope in God is the great hope for the prisoners. It is the hope that God will allow them to survive each day and perhaps get out of jail someday, pick up the pieces in their lives, and start a new chapter.

I met a friend at church and sometimes after service we would talk about family and being a Christian. We were also members of the same gym, so we sometimes see each other during our early morning workouts. One day, we started talking about jail ministry. He seemed very interested and was asking me lots of questions about it. He later confided in me that he had been an inmate in jail earlier in his life. He said that Christian volunteers would come into jail and share God's word with them, and that he would attend these bible studies in jail. Over time, he became a Christian and God started changing his life. When he got released from jail, he met a wonderful woman and eventually married her. God gave him a good job and a loving family with children. He and his family now regularly attend church together. He said he will always be thankful to the people who came into jail and helped lead him to God. I had the privilege of seeing the result of his transformed life and how beautiful it was. Jail was the turning point in his life because God met him there. It was good for me to see both sides: the reality of the locked up inmates as contrasted with the freedom of a former inmate who now lives the life that God always had intended for him. When Jesus was arrested as an innocent man, He felt the loneliness and isolation of a prisoner being forcibly taken away from His family and friends. Perhaps that's why He commands us not to forget those in prison. Jesus said in *Matthew 25:36-40, "…I was in prison and you came to visit me…I tell you the truth, whatever you did for one of the least of these brothers of mine, you did for me."* Jesus said that when you visit someone in jail, even the lowliest of people, it's the same as visiting Jesus himself. How cool is that! Can you imagine visiting Jesus in jail, the Son of God, the supreme Creator of all things? What an immense honor that Jesus places before us! Since Jesus is able to feel the same emotions that we feel, He understands the crushing effects that loneliness and isolation can have on the inmates. Jesus is such a brilliant communicator that he is able to bring God's commands to a very personal level. Jesus shows us the great value of each individual human life by the way he talked to and interacted with common people. He saw the potential for greatness in people that no one else could see, and He demonstrated this as He chose twelve common fishermen to become His apostles.

I began to understand that some of the inmates may be contemplating suicide. The jail chaplain would brief our group about the warning signs of an inmate that was potentially suicidal. I realized that God may be using me to help prevent an inmate from taking his own life by bringing God's message of love, joy, peace, and hope into jail. Perhaps we could reach out to these inmates, through the power of God, and overturn these thoughts of suicide. I can warmly welcome them into the family of God and tell them about the superlative privileges that go along with it. God offers a new way of life that is so much greater than what the world offers, and I get the privilege of getting to tell them about it. I get to tell them my personal story and how God saved me and continuously pours His grace and mercy upon me and my family. The ultimate prize for a human being is to obtain eternal life in heaven with God and His Son, and God is using me to bring His beautifully precious message to my fellow men and women.

Chapter 15

Eternity For A Mist

Today in jail, we talked about the exquisite gift of eternal life that God offers each one of us. We tried to imagine what the beauty of heaven might be like. Since we have only seen the beautiful places on earth, such as the Hawaiian Islands or one of the National Parks, we thought perhaps heaven would look something like that. God placed the beauty of the Hawaiian Islands on display for all to see what He can do. You have to try really hard to have a bad day in Hawaii. In *Galatians 6:8 it says, "...the one who sows to please the Spirit, from the Spirit will reap eternal life, Let us not become weary in doing good, for at the proper time we will reap a harvest if we do not give up."* Since the Spirit of God lives inside believers, we are guided by His Spirit. If we believe that Jesus is our Savior, we will follow the Spirit of God, and demonstrate our faith in Him, which has a byproduct of good works, and we receive eternal life as a gift from God. Our lives on earth are very brief when we compare them to eternity, so if we give our brief earthly lives to God and follow His Spirit, we gain eternal life in exchange.

There is a line across the walls in the detaining rooms where we gather for Sunday services. To illustrate eternal life, I tell the inmates to imagine that the line from one end of the wall to the other represents all eternity. I then point to a tiny spec at the beginning of the line that would represent each one of our brief lives on earth. "So God says if you give this tiny spec to me by believing in my son, I will give you eternal life." A pretty good deal if you ask me! God always offers us the much better side of an enormously great deal. In fact, this is by far the greatest gift that God offers us, to live all eternity with Him and His Son Jesus forever in paradise! It's interesting that the scripture says not to become weary in doing good. It pleases the Spirit of God when we do good to honor Him. How can we do good? Sometimes when we are in a parking lot or busy shopping area, it's beneficial to pause for a moment and look around us to see how we can do something good in a hectic situation. A smile is a good start. Giving up that parking spot or letting someone get in the checkout line in front of us can be a good gesture. A warm greeting or some friendly words can go a long way in helping make someone else's day a little better. Being joyful can show the world that we believers are wonderfully different. These are simple things but can be powerful when we do them to honor God. We are different because we have already started living our eternal lives even as we are still walking around on this earth. However, our lives on earth are very brief and in fact are described by James in *James 4:14, "Why you don't even know what will happen tomorrow. What is your life? You are a mist that appears for a little while and then vanishes."* Imagine giving up a mist or a vapor in exchange for eternal life in paradise! How many times have you attended a funeral service where you heard someone say that life is short or that a person's life was very fleeting? Sometimes it takes a funeral service for me to reflect on how brief life on earth can really be. Whenever a friend or loved one passes away, I spend some time to rethink on my life and how I can live it with more wisdom. I recently attended a funeral for a 32-year-old man that I knew from work. He left a one-year-old daughter behind that will never know or remember her father. It was very sad as I watched them lower his casket into the hole in the ground and cover it up with dirt. Someone leaned over to me and said, "Get ready, this is going to happen to all of us." I realized at this moment how much I depend on the trustworthiness of God's promises and hope of life after death. I have to admit that when I am having a particularly bad day I will sometimes think, "Ok God, you can take me today, I'm ready for eternity in Paradise!" but maybe God hasn't finished His work through me yet. I believe that this book is one of my unfinished works. My involvement in jail ministry is another, and I'm sure there are others that I don't even know about yet. I have spoken to the inmates about the importance of doing God's work and the deep fulfillment that comes from completing the work. The sense of purpose is powerful, and we talk about working as a team. I come to jail to teach God's Word and then it spreads as the inmates carry the message to many other inmates deep within the jail from their cells. Don't let your life be an empty waste of time. Please live the remaining part of your life (however much time God gives each one of us) by leaving God's imprint on the world daily. I guarantee that you will live a happier life full of joy and peace, the world needs you!

Chapter 16

God Fills Us With Joy So Act Like It

The definition of joy is "a feeling of great pleasure and happiness." This is one of our regular discussion topics in jail. We talk about the reasons that we and our fellow Christians are to be living a joyful life and why our joy should spill out and overflow to be on display to all of those around us so we can bring glory to our God! Life is fun when God is the focal point! Without Him, life is filled with shallowness and emptiness. It took me many years of marriage and also some years with my children before God revealed to me that my wife and my children are intimately precious gifts to me directly from God Himself. Having a spouse and children to share life with has brought me great joy and also a much needed healthy balance into my life. I now give thanks to God regularly for these enormous gifts He has given me. We must remember to never take these blessings for granted and always treat our spouse as the exquisite gift that they are. Our spouse and children should expect an uplifting experience when they see us each day. Don't be known as a complainer who is always dragging others down with every little problem encountered in life. People will start to avoid us if we are frequently sulking around making people's day worse by constantly griping about life's many trivial shortfalls. As Christians, our joy comes from our relationship with the living God, not from our present situation or our worldly possessions. Our joy comes from knowing that we have inherited eternal paradise from an unfathomable, supernatural God in heaven who, thankfully, happens to be rich in kindness and mercy! This is what John says about joy in *John 15:11 "....I have told you this so that my joy may be in you.."*

When we love God and follow His spirit, God fills us with His joy, and it overflows to the world around us. This is one of the many supernatural gifts that God promises to us. God's joy is remarkably uplifting, in all His attributes and He places within us a desire to share it with others! Joy is contagious! I know that I personally feel better when I can bring joy into someone else's life, maybe helping make their day a little bit better. This comes from our Father. God loves the peacemakers in this world. It's greatly fulfilling to share joy with others: smiling, sharing time and meals together, laughing with friends, having fun together, and celebrating birthdays with close friends and family on a nice day in the backyard. Whenever I have free time, I really enjoy sharing my time with people that are fun and joyful to be with! We can bring Glory to God by telling others that we are joyful because we love our magnificent God. I find that it's healthy to have a good robust sense of humor, not to be easily offended by those around us. I'm also finding that joy comes when we share with others. Sharing our backyards with friends and neighbors, watching their children innocently playing in the swimming pool, splashing and having fun on a hot summer day and sharing meals or coffee with neighbors and friends are all ways to spread joy. The inmates experience joy when they share what little resources they have with others such as candy or some food or reading scripture together with cell mates. It unites all of us as family when we share joy with one another. Joy breaks down barriers and brings families, neighborhoods, and communities closer together as all of us experience the journey through this precious life that God has given us. I also experience joy when I am truly and passionately thankful to God and express my gratitude towards Him for all the wonderous blessings that He has graciously bestowed on me and my family. It's so amazing that we worship a God that loves to give gifts and blessings to His children! God gives us life's recipe for joy and contentment in His written word to us and also gives us His Holy Spirit to help us experience the best in this life. I personally find it to be a calming and peaceful experience when I read His words in the Bible, a book so beautifully and elegantly written through supernatural inspiration.

Examples of daily Joy

-   Loving our living God

- Marveling over His creation
- Hugging and kissing our spouse good morning
- Embracing and talking to our children
- Enjoying a great meal with others
- Spending time outdoors walking or hiking
- Spending the day at a river or lake
- Riding a bike
- Working on a hobby you enjoy
- Listening to music
- Laughing with a friend
- Watching the beauty of a sunrise
- Spending time at the beach
- Hosting a barbecue
- Swimming in a pool
- Watching our children achieve major milestones in life

Chapter 17

The Christmas Story

Christmas is an intensely emotional time of year for the inmates when they feel the true reality of the deep isolation that they are facing in jail. The volunteers put together Christmas bags that get handed out in jail on Christmas Eve every year that contain a small Bible and some gifts. Sometimes the inmates, no matter how hardened their outer appearance may be, emotionally break down and cry because that small Christmas bag is the only gift they received that year, and they are touched that anyone has cared about them. I always share what I call the "Christmas Story" with them in the month of December, which comes from the biblical accounts and the historical events that encompass and describe the birth of our Lord and Savior Jesus Christ. This is one of the most astounding and historically significant events in all human history. Our superior, supernatural Creator stepped off the perfection of His throne in paradise. He emptied Himself to step down to our dark world and lowered Himself even further by becoming a human baby that was born outdoors in poverty and utter humility and laid in a manger (an animal feeding trough) at night in the small obscure village of Bethlehem in Judea. Why would an ultra-supreme all-powerful and glorious God do such a thing? It turns out that God's motivation has always been His deep passionate love for us. *John 3:16 says, "For God so loved the world that He gave His one and only Son, that whoever believes in Him shall not perish but have eternal life."* He came to earth to eat, sleep, drink, and walk with us humans as He taught us how to live our lives to the fullest, directly from the ultimate authority of all creation. Jesus could have been born into a rich family and had all the finest things in life as well as great political influence, but instead, God preferred Him to be born into lowly status. Interestingly enough, the Christmas story that I present to the inmates starts with the first passage and first three words in the Bible, *Genesis 1:1 "In the beginning".* It's quite remarkable that about 1,000 years after Moses wrote Genesis, the New Testament book of John also starts with the same 3 words, *John 1:1 "In the beginning".* There is an interesting correlation between the two biblical accounts. Genesis focuses on God's creation of the earth, life, and universe, while John's account gives great detail on who God was with and the role of His son Jesus during the creation of all of existence. *John 1:1 says, "In the beginning was the Word, and the Word was with God and the Word was God. He was with God in the beginning. Through Him all things were made; without Him nothing was made that has been made. In Him was life, and that life was the light of men. The light shines in the darkness, but the darkness has not understood it."*

As an eternal being, Jesus always existed, and God and His son Jesus created all things together as a Father/Son team. The Holy Spirit was also present and active during creation. It has always been difficult for me to comprehend that the Son of God, in whose presence the Angels cover their faces (*Isaiah 6*), would willingly lower and empty Himself to transform into a human baby. Jesus came to earth into the darkness of sin, but many people did not understand who He was or what He was doing as stated by the Apostle John. The Prophet Isaiah amazingly foretold the birth of Jesus over 700 years before Jesus was born. *Isaiah 9:6-7 says, "For to us a child is born, to us a son is given, and the government will be on His shoulders. And He will be called Wonderful Counselor, Mighty God, Everlasting Father, Prince of Peace. Of the increase of his government and peace there will be no end. He will reign on David's throne and over his kingdom."* Jesus stepped away from ultimate perfection in paradise, where He was in constant worship by angels, to come to this tiny planet of earth to live life with a bunch of rebellious and violent sinners, who in the end, tortured and murdered Him, our glorious Savior. To try to grasp this transformation, it would be like a human lowering itself to become an insect. This is the magnitude of what Jesus did to become a human baby. God gave His son to the world as a gift for 33 years, the most unbelievable and magnificent gift ever given. I have two sons and I miss them after a few weeks if I can't see them. God was physically separated from His son for 33 years. I can't imagine how much they must have missed each other. The angel Gabriel appeared to Mary in advance and foretold the greatest birth that ever took place in *Luke 1:31, "You will be with child and give birth to a son, and you are to give Him the name Jesus. He will be great and will be called the Son of the Most High."* The ancient Magi (wise men) realized the colossal significance of the birth of the Creator of the universe as stated in *Matthew 2:1-2, "…Magi from the east came to Jerusalem and asked, Where is the one who has been born king of the Jews? We saw his star in the east and have come to worship Him."* Instead of making a great public announcement, God chose to reveal the birth of His son privately to the humble shepherds in the field. *Luke 2:10-14 says, "But the angel said to them "…I bring you good news of great joy that will be for all the people. Today in the town of David a Savior has been born to you; he is Christ the Lord" Luke 2:13-15 Suddenly a great company of the heavenly host appeared with the angel and saying "Glory to God in the highest and on earth peace to men on whom His favor rests." When the angels had left them and gone into heaven, the shepherds said to one another " Lets go to Bethlehem and see this thing that has happened, which the Lord has told us about."* The inmates are astounded and astonished at the lengths and measures that God and Jesus went through for us sinners, who frankly don't deserve anything. The King of Kings came to the earth as a baby and changed the course of history forever. This little baby grew up and lived a sinless life that defeated sin, Satan, and death itself so that all of us can have a chance to live with Him and God the Father in peace for all of eternity in paradise. His message of love and peace is so powerful that even today it motivates many people, as well as the inmates, to live their lives completely different. I want to live a life that brings glory to God, by loving Him as well as my neighbors, and I urge those in jail to do the same. The inmates realize that living life their own way has caused a trail of great pain and regrets but living life God's way offers a refreshing new path that leads to peace and great joy and eternity in heaven with an indescribable God.

Chapter 18

Is Following Jesus Easy?

The answer is simply "no". Following Jesus always has been and will continue to be difficult, but I can guarantee it's worth it! Jesus' life has always been motivated by His love for us and for His Father. His passionate love is what drove Him to do everything He did, including all the miracles. This passion is what drove Him to freely hand over His life to a horrendous and tortuously brutal death. This is what Jesus said about following Him in *Luke 9:23, "If anyone would come after me, he must deny himself and take up his cross daily and follow me. For whoever wants to save his life will lose it, but whoever loses his life for me will save it."* Jesus commands us to deny ourselves as well as sacrifice and suffer daily if we want to follow Him. This is not just giving up something during the 40 days of lent, or giving up meat on Fridays, but instead, sacrificing every day out of love for our eternal God and His son Jesus, which means 365 days a year. Jesus says that we must submit our earthly lives to Him if we want to save our lives for all of eternity. Jesus also said that if your live life for yourself, you will lose it for all eternity. Again, my daily sacrifice and suffering does not earn my way into heaven but is merely an affirmation that I believe in the living God and that His Son Jesus is my Savior. It also signifies that we are worthy of following Him. However, I have found that I actually enjoy my daily sacrifices and suffering for my God because He created me, and I have the highest level of respect, fear, and love for Him. When I'm sacrificing for God, it reminds me to humble myself before His unimaginable, brilliant majesty and splendor. I also achieve a feeling of inner peace and joy when I suffer and sacrifice for God, which is very therapeutic for my soul. Jesus also said in *Matthew 10:38, "and anyone who does not take his cross and follow me is not worthy of me"*. Again, Jesus reminds us to take up our cross which is not easy, but it's a vital investment to demonstrate our worthiness in following him. These daily sacrifices are reminders of who God is and the love, honor, and respect He deserves.

CPSIA information can be obtained
at www.ICGtesting.com
Printed in the USA
BVHW052109070223
658071BV00011B/233